SHOCKS NO MORE!
From Surviving... to Thriving

Dr. Kim R. Tousignant

All Rights Reserved

2016

Published in the United States of America

by Author, Dr. Kim Tousignant

Bucksport, Maine

ISBN: 978-0-9976882-0-7

$8.95 USA.

SHOCKS NO MORE!
From Surviving . . . to Thriving

Incoming Information	1
Adverse Childhood Experiences	2
Dr. Seligman's Research	4
Stuck in the Box	5
Control, Power, Safety	7
In Danger We React	8
Learned Helplessness	9
Getting Out of the Box	11
Feeling Nothing (Dissociation)	12
Shock = Shatter Like Glass	13
Flashbacks	14
Ultimate Wish	15
Things People Do to Control Their Shocks	17
Control in Life: Adults	19
Control in Life: Children	21
Paradigm Shift: A New Approach	23
The Most Difficult Thing You Will Ever Do!	25
Anxiety With Change	26
Stages of Change	27
Pain and Waiting for Next Shock	28
External vs Internal Locus of Control	29
Explosion of the Overstuffed Closet	30
What Does Your Behavior Mean to You?	32
The Take Away	33
References	34

INCOMING INFORMATION

Generally, information is taken into our brains and processed, organized and filed right away so we can retrieve it easily through language. This is the "intellectual" side* of the brain. The rational, logical, unemotional side.

But when something is happening that threatens our well-being we must react quickly and there isn't time for all that processing. So the information goes into our brain DIFFERENTLY. It bypasses the language side and goes straight into the "emotional," reactive, non-verbal side.

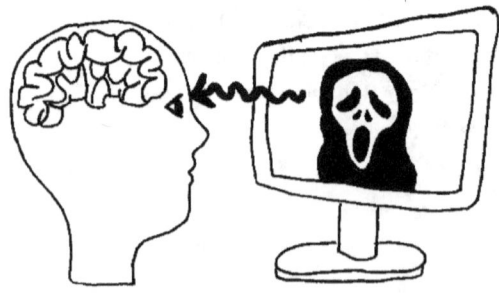

---

*The brain has 2 sides (hemispheres). Generally the left side is the intellectual side and the right is the emotional side. But in at least 10% of the population it is the opposite, and this is often dependent on a person's dominant hand.

The body chemicals released during a threat actually cause changes in our brain structure too. It follows then, that this information continues to influence us in ways that are not connected to our language and intellectual understanding! Have you ever felt like crying but don't know why? Then struggled to explain in words what you are feeling? This is because that experience did not go through the word center of your brain so it's really hard for it to come out that way!

ADVERSE CHILDHOOD EXPERIENCES

If YOU have experienced multiple Adverse Childhood Experiences (ACEs) (Felitti, V. J., et al. (1998)) such as trauma, neglect, abuse, instability, chaos, a catastrophe, an accident, a crime, and/or witnessed domestic violence, it is possible that as an adult you continue to experience unpredictability, chaos, dysfunction and or trauma. If so, it is possible you suffer from Learned Helplessness and don't even know it! Let's explore what that is and how you might heal in order to better accomplish your life goals.

When I studied Psychology I made a commitment to not participate in any research that would cause harm to animals. I love animals and want research with animals to be a last resort only in special circumstances. I want to warn you that this study can be upsetting because of how animals were treated. In this situation I believe what we learned was worthwhile.

DR. SELIGMAN'S RESEARCH

In the 1960's Dr. Martin Seligman (Seligman, M. E., Maier, S. F., & Geer, J. H. (1969). Current Position: Zellerbach Family Professor of Psychology Director, Positive Psychology Center through University of Pennsylvania, Philadelphia, Pennsylvania) used dogs to study learning theory about punishment. The experiment was designed somewhat like this
<small>(Please NOTE: I have taken some creative liberty with the model to help us understand the points that are most important to you)</small>

So, let's say there are 2 dogs..........
> Each dog was put in a separate box;
> 1 box had a cover, the other didn't.
> Each box was wired to produce a shock
> *when the experimenter chose.*
> When a shock hit the box <u>without a cover</u>
> <small>(green box to left)</small> the dog could escape quickly.
> When a shock hit the box <u>with a cover locked on</u>
> <small>(red box to left)</small> the dog was *trapped* and escape was *impossible.*

The experimenters came to wonder..........
> *"What will the trapped dog do* <small>(red box to left)</small>
> *if a shock is delivered*
> *with the cover removed?"*

Do YOU think the dog, that was first trapped, escaped the shocks by jumping out of the box when the cover was off?

No!

The dogs, who were first trapped in the box, did not learn
- on their own -
to jump out of the box!

All behavior has a function or reason that it is done.

What do you think keeps the dog from escaping the shocks in the box?

Why would the dog stay in that horrible situation and not just leave the box?

CONTROL, POWER, SAFETY

Everyone tries to understand what they personally did to make something happen; *good* (positive) or *bad* (negative).

We want to learn how to have good things happen again & again.

And we want to learn to prevent bad things from happening.

People sometimes ask:
> *"What did I do to deserve a SHOCK?"*
> *"How is my behavior related to the SHOCK?"*
> *"How will I know when a SHOCK will happen again?"*
> *"What can I do to make the SHOCKS stop?"*

But........ what if your behavior has NOTHING to do with the actions of others towards you, like the shocks to the dogs? They did NOTHING wrong to deserve being shocked. Rather, the shock has everything to do with the person doing the shocking. The dog won't be able to figure out a pattern because the dog is NOT IN CONTROL of the shocks. The shocks then are unpredictable, have no explanation, and that leaves the dog confused, helpless and hopeless!

When people are confronted with a dangerous situation there are things we do to try to stay safe:

> # IN DANGER WE REACT
>
> ## 1. Seek Help From Others
> If others are not available to help we:
> ## 2. Flee (flight)
> Run away from the problem.
> ## 3. Fight
> Fight the problem head on.
> If 1-3 don't work we:
> ## 4. Freeze
> Once we learn that <u>our behavior has no effect on the outcome</u> we shut down thinking 'Why try?' and our body freezes.

Biology has a way to prepare a body to experience less trauma by shutting down. It shuts down mental connection with the outside world, then systems begin to shut down-like going into shock after an accident.

In a situation where a person is trapped, if they try using strategies 1, 2 or 3 above, it might even result in more harm and less likelihood of survival!

Turn the page for some reasons people might stay in an unhealthy place where they feel trapped. →

LEAVE???

Nah, I will just stay here.

If it is this bad here – how much worse will it be out there?

It is familiar.

It is all I know.

I know what to expect here.

I'm used to it.

I know how to handle it.

I'm too stressed.

I can't handle changes.

It was good enough for me.

It is just the way life is....

So, how <u>DID</u> the experimenters eventually get the dogs to leave, the boxes delivering the shocks, of their own free will?

    Calling the dog out happily?   NO!
    Watching another dog leave the box?   NO!
    Tasty treats or other rewards?   NO!

All the skills the dogs had and knew to use wouldn't get them out of the box! It was like they were FROZEN in their spot. This is **<u>Learned Helplessness.</u>**

The dogs were made helpless by being trapped, through no fault of their own. But when the situation changed they didn't understand they could now escape without help. Fear overwhelmed them. Being trapped led them to generalize "I really am helpless, not just in this situation but everywhere!"

The experimenters found only one solution to get the dogs, with Learned Helplessness, to leave the box on their own.

Experimenters had to physically pick up the dogs AND move their legs showing the dogs the movements they needed to make to leave the box . . . . But . . . . .

GETTING OUT OF THE BOX

Once wasn't enough! The dogs had to be shown <u>at least 2 times</u> how to get out before they began escaping the shocks by leaving the box on their own!

In Van der Kolk's latest book, <u>The Body Keeps the Score</u>, the first chapter has some amazing MRI pictures. One person's reaction to a bad car accident was that they "felt nothing" and the brain scan showed literally almost no brain activity:

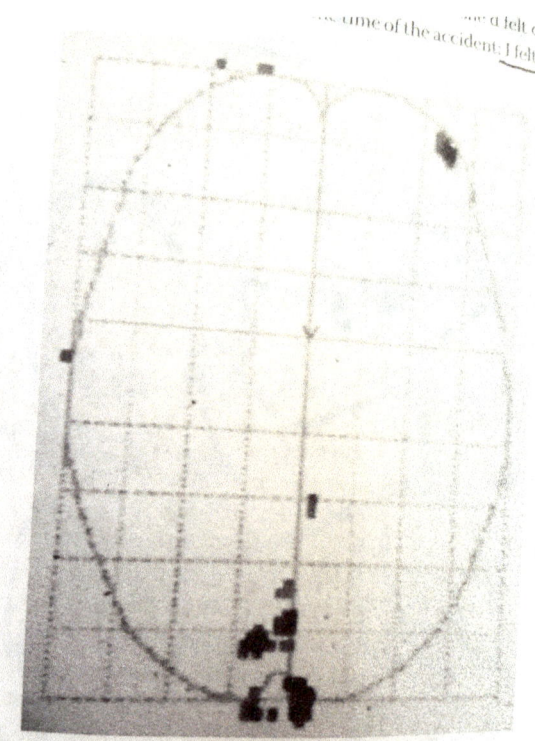

Blanking out (dissociation) in response to being reminded of past trauma. In this case almost every area of the brain has decreased activation, interfering with thinking, focus, and orientation.

Van der Kolk B (2014). *The body keeps the score. Brain, mind, and body in the healing of trauma.* Penguin copyright photo Permission Granted 4/7/16 Contract #522701

There is a very strong adaptive function in the body when it "feels nothing." If the body is experiencing trauma (emotional and/or physical) by "feeling nothing" the person can disengage from the debilitating pain. Disengaging slows down the heart, breathing and digestive systems, reduces awareness and even reduces physical pain. In essence, the body is preparing to die without the horrific pain that would otherwise be there. Animals also do this. The emotional experience of "feeling nothing" is called **Dissociation.**

In order to help pull someone out of dissociation they have to learn to become alert and engaged. They already know how to disengage!

We have seen how actual shocks affect dogs that are trapped. Let's look at the metaphor of a SHOCK in terms of people. Any experience that a person perceives (their own personal experience) as being hurtful, harmful, not fulfilling a need, or traumatic can be considered a SHOCK. It can be something huge - losing a dream job, or relatively small - having a date cancelled. People who have had Adverse Childhood Experiences may react to a SHOCK differently than someone who grew up with a solid foundation from which to encounter the world.

This is my image of the internal feelings a person (with multiple ACEs in their past) experiences when SHOCKS come in today, even when they are no longer trapped. →

SHOCK = SHATTER LIKE GLASS

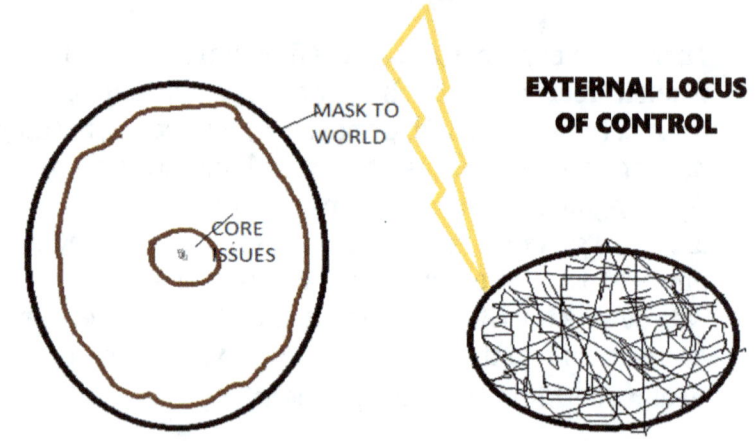

Core Issues: Powerlessness, Abandonment, fear, unlovable, unworthy, helpless, victim, hopeless, hostile world view, people will hurt me, people won't be there for me, I know there will be a bomb, waiting for it to drop, meant to be unhappy, destined to be miserable

First, look at the circle on the left. The <u>solid outside circle</u> represents the mask traumatized people feel they need to wear for the world; the "everything is fine" mask.

Inside, however, their "normal" feelings are vulnerable & fragile (the crooked line). They engage the world, hoping no one will discover they are broken on the inside.

I believe everyone has a Core Issue or two that will present lifelong learning opportunities. Those with multiple ACES may have more.

Now, look at the circle on the right. This is what it FEELS like when a "SHOCK" comes in from the outside. Intense waves of emotional pain and helplessness engulf the whole sense of self so that it feels like one's being has truly shattered like glass and it feels like nothing can stop this feeling. It's as if the EXTERNAL world is controlling their emotional life (External Locus of Control).

When an internal Core Issue is triggered or pushed, the reaction is much bigger than perhaps it would have been if there had been no history of Adverse Childhood Experiences. The intensity of feeling is beyond words. And the person feels like they will _TRULY DIE/Shatter_ from each SHOCK.

When the shock hits the internal Core Issue, the feelings related "to today's situation" combine with those overwhelming feelings from when trapped and helpless. Sometimes it feels like one has been teleported right back into that previous moment in time--as if they are there reliving the experience. This is a **Flashback.**

And flashbacks are interesting in that they can take many forms. Some might be visual so that one can see in their mind's eye an event from their past being intensely relived-this is the typical explanation of a flashback. However, each 5 bodily senses can produce flashbacks independently. For example, you get a pain in your back & don't know why, and doctors find nothing. Perhaps you fell on your back during an abuse situation, and something triggered your brain to remember that fall, thus your back hurts. Or you suddenly feel like crying and don't know why. You may have unknowingly been triggered by something and your knowledge of that event has been cut off from your emotions (dissociation).

Let's go back to thinking about our stuck dog.

IF a fairy were to come down and grant the dog 1 ultimate wish in life what do you think it might be?

My SHOCKS NO MORE! theory is that the dog's ultimate wish would be to CONTROL the shocks.

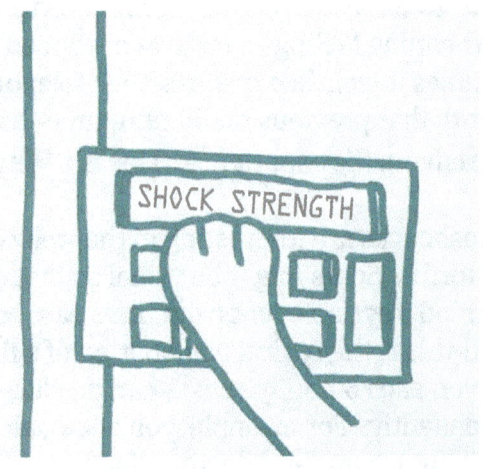

This is different than the initial impression of people. Remember, the cover was off but the dog did not leave the box, so that's not the goal. And now that the dog expects shocks (not related to their behavior) they expect there will always be shocks, so turning the shocks off wouldn't be it either.

Can you believe experimenters discovered that people would prefer to electrically shock themselves instead of being left alone with their own thoughts! (Wilson, T.D., Reinhard, D. A., Westgate, E. C., Gilbert, D. T., Ellerbeck, N., Hahn, C., Brown, C. L. & Shaked, A., 2014)

So while the dogs really were in boxes, people are (generally) not really in a box. The box is an imaginary way to organize our thinking of patterns in behavior. Do you ever wonder why you keep doing the same thing over & over, even though each time the results are not what you want? Repeating thoughts & behaviors over & over is a way people, who feel helpless, seek to gain **Mastery.**

By taking control over the shocks it "feels" powerful, even if just an illusion. The person feels control is gained, over some aspect of life.

For example:
> If a child is abused at home they may become a bully at school. Even they don't like being abused or hurting others. It is true they "feel" powerful (identification with the abuser) over violence, but I view this as "stolen power." I believe true power should be earned through respect. Immersion in violent video games is another form of building illusory mastery.

Sometimes, repetitive behaviors appear to have nothing to do with the actual behaviors that couldn't be controlled when trapped. The patterns can be substitutes - things you might really be able to have control over. For example - you might need to wash your hands a lot, otherwise you feel a lot of anxiety.

What do YOU think are the kinds of patterns or behaviors people do to "attempt to control their SHOCKS"? (*Try to write some down before moving on!*)

OCD
reckless driving
say mean things
Addictions
TAKE THE FIGHT "BAIT"

hasty decision
trying to fix something that is not yours
try to squeeze a square peg in a round hole
choosing similar partners
"I always screw it up"

start a fight
quit job   impulsive move
"but I love him/her"
compulsive shopping
taking on others problems as your own

"WHY DO I DO THESE THINGS?"

To the left are just some of the things people do to control the SHOCKS in their lives. The patterns can be in the things and/or ways you:
    think   say
    feel   do (or don't do)
    interact with others

For example:
    Sometimes it can feel like the only way out of emotional pain is to think about suicide. You realize: "If I am the one who decides if I live or die I am the one in control." Pretty soon the thought can seem to "automatically" appear with any kind of emotional pain; small or huge. This has become a thinking habit. You may not really want to be dead, but you want the miserable pain to go away.

What patterns might YOU have developed to control the SHOCKS in your life? *(feel free to jot down notes here if you like)*

THE REALITY OF CONTROL IN LIFE: ADULTS

I have used the term "control" often in this discussion. We all know about concepts such as "free will," the right to make our own decisions, etc. But do we really have FULL-100% control over our lives?

It is my personal opinion that Adults have, *at most*, 80% control over their lives. Some believe it is a lot less! So that leaves about 20% of adult life we have absolutely no control over.

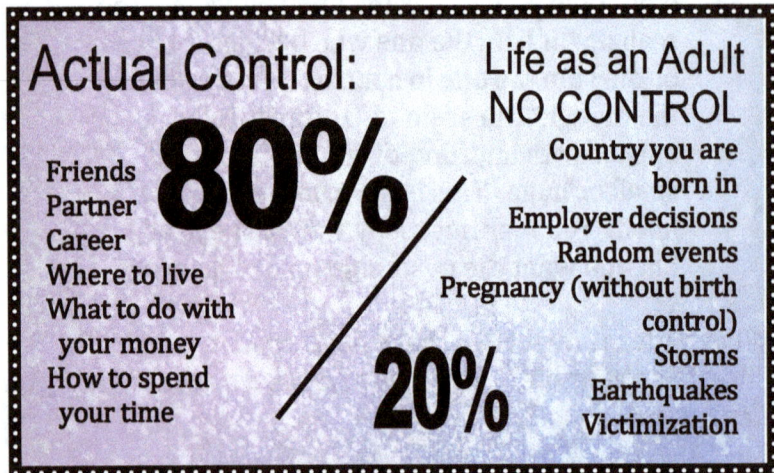

For example:

    Think about a random trauma- Say, lightning hits a person (now that's the most literal form of a shock!). The person then begins to fear any situation that may present the possibility of lightning. And they restructure their lives so it won't happen again. But, no matter how hard they try to prevent/avoid another lighting strike, is it possible it might happen again? Statistically --of course it could happen again. Restructuring life to avoid any possibility of lightning is essentially developing life around your fears.

I call this "living in your 20%." As an adult you get to decide where you devote your time and attention. Are you going to choose to live your life stuck in constant fear with abnormal reactions to avoid the 20% of life you don't have any control over? Or are you going to choose to live within the 80% of your life where you have real control?

Those 20% moments, where you have (had) absolutely no control, can dramatically affect your life.

For example:
>Say a friend is hit by a drunk driver (completely out of their control) who crossed the yellow line and the friend loses a limb. This will affect the rest of their life! So how can they possibly let go of that?

The person can <u>choose to radically accept</u> that it might happen again - BUT... they are smart about it; they develop a safety plan to recognize what they do and don't have control over. They develop ways to prevent a reoccurrence. They know and can use a set of actions should it happen again. Then they choose to TRUST IN THEMSELVES that they will do their best should another moment like that occur.

I have a question for you to consider before you turn the page. Is this 80/20 split the same for children?

THE REALITY OF CONTROL IN LIFE: CHILDREN

No!

Children do NOT get to choose their living environment! So, their experience is VERY different. I think of the percentage being switched: a child has, *at most,* 20% control and **80% LACK of Control**.

If you have children in your care, it is important to remember that the children's welfare must guide your decision-making process.

For example:
>If there are no children living in the home,
>>*you can choose to stay
>>in an abusive or toxic relationship
>>if you feel the pros outweigh the cons.*

>But what if there are children in the home?
>>*if you provide an environment where
>>children are exposed to Adverse Events,
>>YOUR CHILDREN may also develop
>>Learned Helplessness.*

Research proves Learned Helplessness and similar problems pass from one generation to the next. So, ideally, adults would do EVERYTHING within their power to protect children from Adverse Childhood Events and/or being trapped in a harmful environment. You must REMEMBER however, there are things out of adult's control and preventing ACEs is not always possible (80/20).

Can you make a list of the things in your life you actually have control over, versus have "no control" over?

My Life:

Actual Control	No Control
	(psst. this includes other people!)

PARADIGM SHIFT: A New Approach

You are probably reading this booklet because YOU want change and are willing to make changes. If you are realizing that you, too, are living in a box of dysfunction, it is important to understand that unless your goals help you to jump out of the box onto a different path, you probably won't see the success you are after. Because, if you suffer Learned Helplessness, it is possible that your view of goals could be similar to that stuck dog's ultimate goal– to learn better control of your SHOCKS. In other words, you hope to feel happier from within your "box" of SHOCKS, because the idea of leaving the box has not even been within your awareness of possibility. Many people don't even realize they are living in a "box" until they learn about this theory!

REMEMBER, as an adult, YOU are the MASTER of YOUR world and YOU get to be the one who decides if YOU stay in or jump out of YOUR box.

There are a lot of things for YOU to consider in making this decision about changes and goals. Ideally, YOUR decisions come from thoughtful consideration with all the information about possibilities, rather than being a knee-jerk reaction out of anger/fear or some other feeling you are trying to avoid from your past.

Growth is not generally a matter of spinning harder or faster. It requires a **NEW APPROACH**: A paradigm shift.

Your Goals.
Your Dreams.
Your Vision.
YES! You can do it!

SO..... JUMPING out of the box is EASY you say?

WRONG!

....it is the hardest & scariest thing a person will ever do in their lives! If being in the box is this awful- how horrible could it be out there in the whole wide world where you <u>don't know</u> what it looks like, or what to expect? You may think:

"The box may not be healthy, but it is at least familiar & comfortable & I know what to expect."

Moving outside the box takes time, practice and can cause tremendous anxiety.

For example:

Consider "Bob" grew up in chaos and has never really lived for an extended period of time in calmness. He is actively engaged in making life changes and he sees his life really is changing! Its calmer with much less drama. And he likes it. Then, suddenly, his anxiety skyrockets! He feels nervous and tense inside. It may even feel worse than when he 1st started making changes. This is tremendously scary for Bob and he's sure he "just wasted all that time making changes" because now Bob is worse than before. Bob panics feeling this is the bomb "I knew would drop." He is convinced he has back-tracked, and is sure "this is the evidence that there really is no hope for me to get better."

BOB IS VIEWING HIS ANXIETY ALL WRONG!!!

I cannot stress how important it is for Bob to understand what his anxiety REALLY MEANS.

It means he is doing something new and, in fact, that he is growing, and doing the work of changing!!

You should expect, as your life changes and you replace unhealthy patterns with healthy ones, that it will create NEW feelings. Just like learning anything new, in the beginning there is nervousness, uncertainty and just plain fear. You can, and *WILL*, learn to be comfortable in this new world, that truly may present you with wonderful gifts you never even imagined!

"Pretty soon, with time, it will feel familiar and predictable and safe and healthy!"

Prochaska & DiClemente (1983) researched how people changed both inside and outside of therapy. They developed their Transtheoretical Approach, which incorporates the Stages of Change, based upon their findings. I have clarified the Stages of Change in terms of the SHOCKS NO MORE! model.

Below is a concrete way for you to envision how to achieve change. These concepts help us understand what growth looks like and what we need to do to find it.

STAGES OF CHANGE

Modeled after Prochaska and DeClemente

1. PRECONTEMPLATION
You don't understand you are living in a box.
You think life is going along normal and 'fine'.

2. CONTEMPLATION
You understand you are in a metaphorical box, realize there is something else out there but are not ready to make any changes.

3. PREPARATION
You are preparing to get out of the box. You want it. You can see it. You have to learn how to get out. You need to practice.

4. ACTION
You are doing whatever it takes to make the changes, no matter how expensive in time, energy, money, etc.

5. MAINTENANCE
Keeping the changes in place even when the uncertainty of life takes hold (stress, trauma etc.)

PAIN AND WAITING FOR THE NEXT SHOCK

Now, let's return to the concept of Core Issues. When a SHOCK comes from the outside, into a person with multiple ACEs, a core insecurity is retriggered by today's struggle. The person can feel as if their world is shattering like glass. They feel shaky, fragile, insecure, afraid and alone. It can feel like they are ping-ponging from one shattering event to the next (we can see ping-ponging triggers between family members too!) and each moment is spent waiting for the next SHOCK; because they "know" it is right around the corner. Encountering the world from this state of **Hypervigilance** (excessively alert to the tiniest of indicators that you might not be safe) is truly miserable, painful and exhausting! It leaves no energy to thrive in life.

It is often exactly this pain that led you to seek change. And most folks are afraid of this pain. But pain (emotional and physical) has an important purpose. Pain informs us that something isn't right and helps guide us towards change and thus growth. Please know, that by reading this booklet YOU are taking a step towards recovering from your pain and moving out if it!

I wish I could promise all kinds of positive results that mean there will be no more trauma or life struggles. Unfortunately, the only thing I can really promise is that you will encounter struggles again in your life. Hopefully, you will have fewer struggles. And you will encounter them with the strength and confidence to know you are doing your very best in that moment! With the ability to accept your choices/actions are good enough. This is encountering the world from an Internal Locus of Control perspective.

MAKING CHANGES

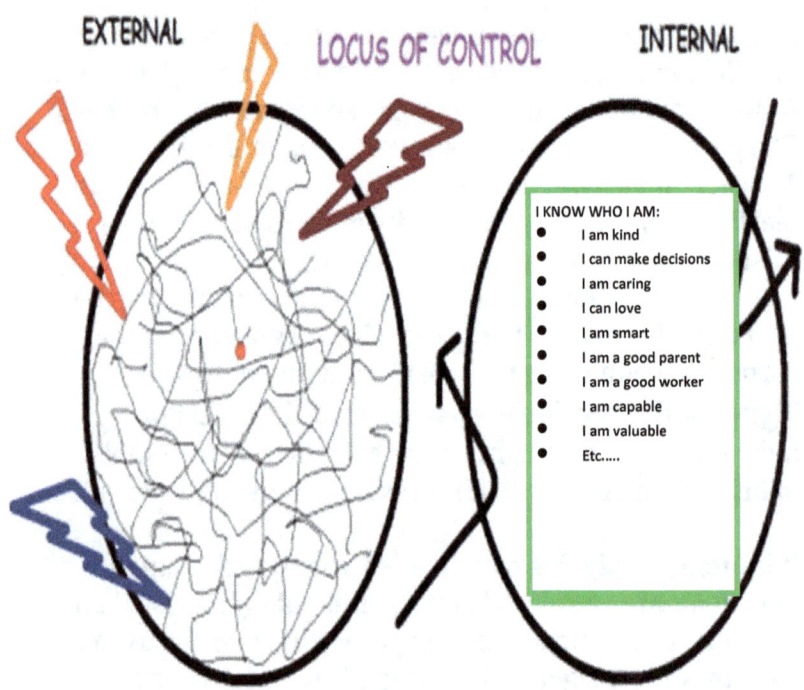

The SHOCKS NO MORE! vision of INTERNAL LOCUS OF CONTROL (LOC) is the circle on the right. Through emotional growth you will learn to trust in yourself. When you have an Internal LOC you know your strengths –realistically. This creates a solid foundation upon which you can walk through your world. And you can rely on that foundation to guide you through the storms of life. You will still have SHOCKS come in- they may still sting, or leave a bruise, maybe even break a bone– but..... they will bounce back out. This is far away from the misery of shattering over & over again.

EXPLOSION OF THE OVERSTUFFED CLOSET

"Let it Go." " Fugettaboutit." "Leave it alone." "That's in the past." "Sweep it under the rug."

Standard reactions are to avoid the things that are hard, because they make us miserable. But if you are like a lot of people, these things just won't stay in the background! Think of it as walking by an overstuffed closet where things are constantly popping out unexpectedly. They just keep bursting through no matter how hard you try to hold them back. AND, they periodically EXPLODE! The door flies open and everything floods you. You may make bad choices, have an outburst of yelling or hitting, lay in bed depressed, feel suicidal or even try to harm yourself.

People, understandably, want to stop this process. Most of my clients have said they would like to throw their difficult and traumatic past away! You CAN NOT throw your past away. Rather, you can figure out what is negatively influencing the present that you would like to change. By processing it and owning it, you can free yourself from being "driven" to do the same unhealthy

thing over and over. Instead you have the emotional freedom to make deliberate decisions that match your values and goals for life.

I call this "cleaning it up." Organizing and straightening the closet, putting your past in the back of the closet so it influences you less than 10% of the time. You know where to find it if you need it; but you rarely have to see it. For example:

> I have 3 plastic tubs of my mementos. I don't take them out very often but they are the first things I would save in a fire! Knowing they are there is a true comfort.

When you do get triggered and that 10% pops up, you immediately know what it is. Your whole sense of self doesn't shatter and crumble. You feel confident in your ability to manage the situation.

Traumatized people are often afraid that if they start talking about their lives (as in psychotherapy), it will pop open the door, so every horror of their life will come pouring out, and they won't be able to stop it, nor will they be able to function anymore. RELAX, this old style of therapy has proven NOT so helpful! Professionals have found that digging in the past "just because" has been shown to re-traumatize and decrease the ability to function in daily life. The BEST goals seek to improve your daily life functioning first!

You can work to make these changes on your own if you have solid community and/or family supports. However, if you have tried to fix these unpredictable triggers (SHOCKS) that cause you to feel horrible and out of control of your life, and you feel stuck and like it is not working, psychotherapy can help you learn to function better on a daily basis. You don't need to be afraid you have to "share your entire life" before you feel better.

WHAT DOES YOUR BEHAVIOR MEAN TO YOU?

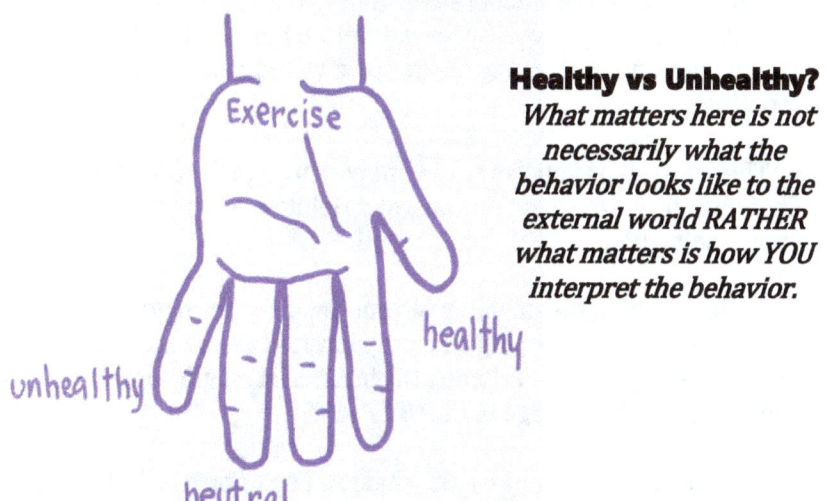

Healthy vs Unhealthy?
What matters here is not necessarily what the behavior looks like to the external world RATHER what matters is how YOU interpret the behavior.

An important component of growth in my SHOCKS NO MORE! Model, is learning about your own behavior. Behaviors can be healthy, unhealthy or neutral. But because behavior can look the exact same on the outside to everyone else, only YOU can determine what a behavior means to you.

Consider drinking water; we often hear how we need to "drink more water, water is healthy." If you are well hydrated, water is a neutral addition to your system. If you are dehydrated drinking water is a healthy behavior. But water can also be very unhealthy- drinking too much after you are already hydrated can throw your electrolytes and system out of whack.

THE TAKE AWAY HERE:

1. It is important to understand if you have been living your life in a box of dysfunction and Learned Helplessness.

2. Then determine the behaviors that keep you in your box, i.e. keep you controlling your shocks.

3. You will have to decide if you want to stay in your box (with the same results, or minor improvements) or if you want to learn how to jump out of the box of your past and create a thoughtful life where you can be deliberate in your choices, instead of reacting and being driven by fears, internal holes, core insecurities and the need to master past victimization through repetition.

4. There are steps you can take to move through the Stages of Change in order to shed your Learned Helplessness method of approaching life.

5. Understanding the meaning of your behavior from your perspective and developing a healthy Internal Locus of Control are key strategies to developing the internal strength to feel confident you can engage in life to THRIVE!

6. If you find you can't make the changes you hope for, seek out a professional counselor/therapist/psychologist that you feel understands you!

7. Keep in mind that counselors, psychotherapists, psychologists and psychiatrists approach treatment from many different models. A good RELATIONSHIP with the therapist is the best predictor of a positive outcome. If you have multiple ACEs a "trauma informed" therapist will help you best. Even then, they might not have an underlying approach that matches this booklet. I have found this approach helps clients grow, and reduces the tension (anger, frustration, confusion) inside therapy. So, if you find this strategy helpful, you might consider sharing it with your own therapist!

REFERENCES

Felitti, V. J., Anda, R. F., Nordenberg, D., Williamson, D. F., Spitz, A. M., Edwards, V., & Marks, J. S. (1998). Relationship of childhood abuse and household dysfunction to many of the leading causes of death in adults: The Adverse Childhood Experiences (ACE) Study. American Journal of Preventive Medicine, 14(4), 245-258.

Norcross, J.C., Krebs, P.M. & Prochaska, J.O. (2011) Stages of Change. Journal of Clinical Psychology: In Session, 67(2) 143-154.

Porges, S. W. (1995). Orienting in a defensive world: Mammalian modifications of our evolutionary heritage. A polyvagal theory. Psychophysiology, 32(4), 301-318.

Prochaska, J.O. & DiClemente, C.C. (1983). Stages and processes of self-change of smoking: Toward an integrative model of change. Journal of Consulting and Clinical Psychology, 51(3), 390-395.

Prochaska, J. O., DiClemente, C. C., & Norcross, J. C. (1992). In search of how people change: applications to addictive behaviors. American Psychologist, 47 (9), 1102.

Rotter, J. B. (1966). Generalized expectancies for internal versus external control of reinforcement. Psychological monographs: General and applied, 80 (1), 1. [This is the initial article on Internal/External Locus of Control. My depiction is not the same.]

Seligman, M. E. (2004). Authentic happiness: Using the new positive psychology to realize your potential for lasting fulfillment. Simon and Schuster.

Seligman, M. E., Maier, S. F., & Geer, J. H. (1968). Alleviation of learned helplessness in the dog. Journal of Abnormal Psychology, 73(3p1), 256.

Van der Kolk, B. (2014). The Body Keeps The Score: Brain, mind, and body in the healing of trauma. Penguin. Photo Permission Granted 4/7/16 Contract # 522701

Wilson, T. D., Reinhard, D. A., Westgate, E. C., Gilbert, D. T., Ellerbeck, N., Hahn, C., Brown, C. L. & Shaked, A. (2014). Just think: The challenges of the disengaged mind. Science, 345(6192), 75-77.

Weiner, Bernard. "Theories of motivation: From mechanism to cognition." (1972).

ART CREDITS

Original Cover Art and Image on Page 28 copyright by Aeriana Blue, Bohemian Dream Art Studio, www.bohemiandream.love.

Hand-drawn Cartoon Art provided by RDesigns1@sbcglobal.com.

Kim Tousignant
Doctor of Psychology

Dr. Tousignant has been in Maine since 2000 and in private practice since 2004. She treats the general population from ages 2-102. She also specializes in treating the disorders that arise from abuse including diagnosing and treating dissociative disorders in children from ages 5 through the elderly. Dr. Tousignant has been working with abused children, their families and adults abused as children since 1980. First as a volunteer, then as an undergraduate at North Carolina State University (Raleigh, NC), where she assisted with chart research on dissociative disorders at Dorothea Dix Hospital through University of North Carolina at Chapel Hill. She earned her M.A. and Psy.D. from Indiana University of Pennsylvania (Indiana, PA). After her pre-doctoral internship at Park Center, Inc. (Fort Wayne, IN), she worked as a DBT therapist and completed a mini-fellowship in Treating Severe Dissociative Disorders through Indiana University (Indianapolis, IN). Dr. Tousignant's dissertation was one of the world's first simultaneous cross-cultural studies in Dissociative Disorders in Two Countries (America and Germany). She wrote (with Dr. Vedat Sar) an international review of dissociative disorders for the International Society for the Study of Dissociation (now ISSTD). Dr. Tousignant's work led to the evolution of this theory. She observes client's growth daily through application of this theory in their lives.

CONTACT

MAILING ADDRESS:
PO Box 1694
Bucksport, ME 04416

PRIMARY OFFICE
151 Main St., Suite 2
Bucksport, ME 04416
(207) 944-8881

FAX: (207) 469-1932

SATELLITE OFFICE
157 Park Street
Suite 22
Bangor, ME 04401
(207) 944-8881

Email: dockimt@gmail.com

drkimtousignant

www.ingramcontent.com/pod-product-compliance
Lightning Source LLC
Chambersburg PA
CBHW070553300426
44113CB00011B/1901